IF YOU REALLY REALLY KNEW ME WOULD YOU STILL IKE 1E?

EUGENE KENNEDY

ARGUS COMMUNICATIONS • NILES, IL 60648

Cover design and
Book illustrations by Gene Tarpey

FIRST EDITION

© Copyright Argus Communications 1975

Printed in the United States of America

ARGUS COMMUNICATIONS
7440 Natchez Avenue
Niles, Illinois 60648

International Standard Book Number 0-913592-51-X
Library of Congress Number 75-34867

     3 4 5 6 7 8 9 0

Contents

CHAPTER ONE

Would Anybody Really Listen

A party is a great place to hide yourself. People clutch their drinks like warriors' shields. Their conversations are like so much winter clothing taken out of storage for the occasion. A lapel cassette player could be used from one party to the next, and nobody would notice.

"We must get together for lunch sometime."

"We're into organic foods this year."

"You've never looked better in your life!"

"I say give them twenty years and they'll solve their own problems."

"I'm on weightwatchers."

"Have you heard the latest about Jackie?"

"Well, the house was just too big for us with the children grown and all."

It is a great game. Everybody talks; nobody listens. You cannot lose because if you do not say anything personal, you cannot get hurt. The rules are simple. Stand in small circles and appear to be listening to each other. It is not surprising that people leave such parties with the feeling they have not been anywhere. Their souls have not been nourished by real contact with other human beings.

Perhaps even sadder, many of these non-listeners are saying to themselves, "I don't even like to listen to myself very much." For although pride and arrogance are called the big sins of the age, most people die of the little ones of self-doubt and insecurity. Too many of us are saying, "I don't see what anybody else could see in me, not if they looked close anyway, not if they knew what I know about myself." Many think not too well but too ill of themselves; they are not overbearing as much as they are underconfident. The bravest of public postures may, after all, mask a private trembling and unsure heart. Little wonder that coolness has become a highly popular way of presenting oneself to others. If I freeze into place, light will not show through the cracks in my facade, and

Coolness
has become
a highly popular way
of presenting
oneself to
others.

the tremor in my knees will not sound so loud. It is not what we show off but what we hide away that tells our truest story.

the uncomfortable self

The fact is that many individuals are not comfortable with themselves, and they spend a great deal of energy trying to keep other people from noticing. It is strange that the very thing they want most of all—simple loving contact with others—they make more difficult because of uncertainty about themselves. They feel they cannot make it on their own merits and so resort to pretending they are somebody else. Is there a fear worse than that which robs one of freedom because he thinks others will not like him? There may be sadder words, wrenched from deeper places in the heart, but few that are spoken so often, perhaps only to themselves, by so many ordinary and good people: "If you really knew me, you wouldn't like me."

Self-consciously they ask themselves, what could anybody else really ever see in them? And how long could they count on the esteem of someone else when they esteem themselves so hesitantly and conditionally?

Better, then, to cover up, to defend against anyone seeing them as they are. Sometimes this is a tactical retreat into a smothering shyness. At other times the defense of the self is accomplished by offense, by a bold and false aggressiveness that keeps others at a distance. Men and women who lack confidence find themselves in a lonely clearing in life. They do not even understand fully that they have hacked their way into this isolation. It is easier to believe that life is unfair or the fates unkind. Easier to believe almost anything but that we are sometimes the uncertain architects of our own loneliness. It is a painful and empty place indeed that we chose to protect ourselves from being hurt in life.

zigzagging through life

Is there a crueler dilemma than that which faces the underconfident? They want to be close, but that opens them to rejection if others get a good look at them; they pull back to spare themselves the wounds of intimacy and thereby intensify their loneliness. People who are uncomfortable with themselves turn to broken-field running to get through life. They are fearful of being too close to others, but are also afraid to be too far away. It is a solution that works and does not work at the same time. But for persons who cannot quite believe in themselves it seems the only way to survive.

Most people do not ask for very much from life. To feel alive they must feel loved. They must sense that somebody else notices and makes room for them, that they measure up in the eyes of somebody else who likes them just as they are. But that seems the impossible dream for those who do not completely like themselves. They do not want to be lost in the crowd, but it at least offers company to their special misery. And so the struggle continues in what is, if we examine it carefully, a very poor solution to the problem of living. There is a special stress involved in trying to live so that somebody special will notice you when you are defending yourself against anybody else noticing you at all.

masks and roles

And you can see this strain in a dozen masks of life, in as many different places, and in enormous variety almost every day. Countless human beings live most of their

**It is not
what we show off
but what we
hide away
that tells
our truest
story.**

lives playing roles. They wear masks they hope will cover up what they dislike about themselves. They harbor the strange hope that they will be liked for what they pretend to be rather than for what they are. That includes the young girl who hides her naiveté with super sophistication as well as the gangster who tries to look like a respectable suburbanite. Count in their numbers the weight lifter who hopes that his muscles will give him the manhood he inwardly questions and the politician who projects a carefully established image to garner applause and votes. These manuevers to capture self-esteem make life resemble a pin-filled war map on which huge armies constantly circle for the best position.

The great American pastime is not sports but the game of looking good and getting liked. The roots of its popularity are deep in the soil of our troubled self-esteem. Are we worth anything and how can we be sure? Many are in doubt and trust neither themselves nor their best instincts. If they could, they would hide unhappily in the shadows forever, their abilities untested, unproven, and unshared. The approval of others is only a second best award, but at least it does not make things worse. It provides a structure—shaky to be sure—in which to carry on.

But this structure is always in danger—the endorsement of others must be sought again every day. It is not a secure thing, this living from the outside in, for our basic feelings about ourselves remain unchanged no matter how much adulation or applause we receive from others. Our weaknesses—or what we fancy weaknesses—may be exposed at any moment. And so we must keep on guard, smiling and posturing now this way and now that, to keep the bubble of our self-esteem from being punctured or just drifting aimlessly away. We never change anything substantially by just altering the externals. We are the same under the makeup and, at some level, we know and fear it. We settle for getting people to like what we let them see, even when it is false, and the basic problem of our self-esteem remains. Living that way creates worry and worse still, robs us of the chance to discover that our true self may be likeable in itself. We may never experience the wonder of being accepted by others even when they have had a good look at us in our worst moments. Our problem is not with the way others view us but with the way we view ourselves. Our difficulties lie not in the untrusting world without but in our own failure to trust what is within. Life is hard enough without our being unnecessarily hard on ourselves. The first, most basic, and most powerful lesson we have to learn is how to like our real selves. Loving ourselves —even if we feel our personalities should be recalled to have their defects fixed—and opening ourselves to life are basic to the development of healthy self-esteem.

listening for ourselves

Would anybody listen if we told the truth about ourselves? We shall never know the truth there is to tell unless we begin to listen to it for ourselves. That is not much to ask for a first step. It is more a call for a cease-fire than a demand for a sudden final victory over ourselves. We need not triumph or surrender. We only need to listen. And if we grant ourselves the double blessing of time and quiet we may begin to hear who we are and what we are really like.

"Would anybody really listen?" The question does not belong only to people at parties. But it is a question that belongs to all

Countless human beings wear masks which they hope will cover up what they dislike about themselves.

of us, and no one can answer it from the out-side. Even to speak the question aloud is a way of hearing and beginning to live by the truth of ourselves.

CHAPTER TWO

Why Do I Hide So Much of Me?

We have heard all this before, but it is still hard to believe in ourselves. We fear that if the truth comes out we might lose our friends. And it is even hard to be friendly to oneself. "Oh, I just could never tell anybody all about myself." Is this a familiar feeling? And why? If we told the truth about ourselves would the world come to an end? Would they have to call out the police? Would our hearts splinter into so many pieces that we could never get them together again?

Sometimes we feel terrible about ourselves but are hard pressed to produce facts that would sustain the indictment we have drawn up against our own character. In a real sense, we can look at ourselves as the worst of sinners, as people with shameful secrets that make us feel deeply guilty to be ourselves. When we do, it is very difficult to look steadily at, much less accept, ourselves. We give ourselves little breathing space or mercy. We make ourselves earn every bit of it. Only grudgingly and partially do we give ourselves permission to live.

Most of us are not psychological show-offs. Showoffs upset those around them in a very special way. The crowd senses that something is wrong when a man or woman works so hard to advertise self. Onlookers feel uneasy, for showoffs generate exactly the opposite reaction from the one they desire. They want to please, to find the combination that will win them the approval they need from others. But rejection greets their awkward, but intensely human, struggle to impress others. Most of us, however, do not cover our insecurity with noise and clamor. We prefer instead to stay well out of the spotlight, in the darkness where our shyness can remain invisible.

Even then we may feel that we are being closely watched by others and struggle to keep up a good front. But we can easily end up acting our way through life, finding the right expressions and learning the correct

If we told the truth about ourselves... would they have to call out the police?

maneuvers that enable us to save face and to look good.

One of the troubles with living this way— aside from the amount of energy it demands —is that it kills our freedom and spontaneity, two of the most important qualities needed for a healthy attitude toward ourselves. We cannot be free when we are bound by the expectations of other people, when being ourselves might meet with disapproval and social failure. We make ourselves miserable when we live as though we were trying to avoid being blackballed at our favorite club. There is not much room left for ourselves—or for even finding out who we are—when impressing others becomes our basic style in life.

Strangely enough, we usually do not hide our bad features. It is often our dirty linen we put on display. Everybody gets to know what is wrong with us; we display our faults well, even though we think otherwise.

But we are often very successful in hiding what is best about us: our talents and strengths, the things that make us special human beings. We get so good at it at times that, despite all our brave talk about marching to different drummers, we blend ourselves completely into the blur of the crowd. We obscure what makes us unique and leave our potential largely unrecognized and untapped. When we get good at it, we can even hide what we can be from ourselves.

We cover up what we are really like because we are uncertain about the way others will value us. Better to hide who we are, we feel, than have ourselves exposed to ridicule, bland indifference, or outright rejection.

parents

Have you ever seen children striving to meet the demands of unrealistic parents? Such children desperately need and want to be loved. They struggle with all their might to find some way to get this response from their parents. And they sometimes bend themselves all out of shape in the process. They strain to match the ideal image their parents have for them, but this means that the truth about themselves is never good enough. Small wonder they never feel good about themselves. These are battered children, not physically, but emotionally. They suffer invisible wounds as they fail in their

21

attempts to please the ones whose love they need.

They may be children, for example, who are only average students, but whose parents have the idea that they should be getting A's and winning first prizes. Children who are viewed in this way at home can never measure up in and of themselves. What they are can never be good enough for the parents who have decided beforehand how wonderful and famous their children must be. It is sad but not surprising that these children find it difficult to get in touch with who they really are, or that they can have lifelong problems of self-confidence and self-esteem.

There are few things more wistful than adults speaking about what they might have been if they had not tried so hard for so long to please somebody else. Living up to someone else's expectations can affect not only your career choice but the kind of marriage you make. Your whole life can take shape around a false notion of who you are. Only later on, and sometimes with great pain, you might discover that you built all your castles in the air, that you are no longer sure what you yourself are really like.

Living up to someone else's expectations can affect not only your career choice but the kind of marriage you make.

the mass media

But it is not just our families or friends who can expect the wrong things from us. The world we live in—that great, brightly-lit 20th century—expects things from us too. Culture often encourages healthy individuality only in theory. There is much talk today of helping people to follow their own stars, of "doing your own thing." A wide variety of products is sold by promising people that their purchase makes them, in one of the greatest cliches of the age, "their own person."

Mass culture, in general, rewards people not for being different but for being alike. It gears its reinforcements to external behaviors rather than to internal attitudes, to what we do far more than to who we are. And, longing for some key to acceptance, we may be easily manipulated into patterning our behavior and sometimes even our values the way business wants them rather than on internal convictions.

The ideals of our culture sometimes urge us to be more like machines than like human beings. We are led to expect popularity if all our parts have the right shape and if they work in perfect harmony; we expect ourselves, machine-like, to perform regularly and unfailingly. Both our brows and hands must remain smooth and unwrinkled as though we had never been involved in either work or worry. Growing old gracefully is almost an impossibility in a culture that regards aging as an unfashionable and almost unpatriotic thing to do. We must disguise what happens to us and, as a result, we cannot understand what is happening to us. Forsake the ''in'' things and we put our popularity in peril. So we often back away from challenging the urgings of mass culture. It is the only place in which we can live and yet it is not deeply satisfying. When we sacrifice too much of our inner selves to gain acceptance, we do not even feel secure because, like fame, popularity can easily be lost. We may end up even more unsure about ourselves, despite our efforts to do all the approved things.

The teachings of culture are not intrinsically wicked, but they are far from wise. They can never produce the feeling of living in depth and in touch with our own selves. How empty is life when it is reduced to all the ''gusto'' you are supposed to be able to grab from a can of beer! How shallow when the self-confidence for falling in love comes out of a toothpaste tube! Life is not much of an adventure when our safety is guaranteed by fixatives for false teeth, our fulfillment by the right toilet paper, our zest for living by the correct softdrink. Nor is there much room for real human companionship when our presence together can only be made possible by products that ensure that never for even an instant will we smell like human beings. There is more to life than this because there is far more to being human than this.

But that is not always easy to see when we are subjected to steady and subtle manipulation. We have to be strong persons to stand out from the crowd in any real sense. That demands self-confidence, the very thing that is being eaten away by a culture that almost force feeds us with glittering but shallow conformity.

the dark cellar

We must look inside ourselves to discover who we are. Ah, but that is just where we do not want to look. Down inside ourselves is the dark place that has scared us before. We hesitate to open the door to the uninviting

Mass culture in general, rewards people not for being different but for being alike.

cellar of the self. We are sometimes frightened by our own impulses, by discovering, for example, that we can feel angry or have sexual feelings at awkward times or in places where we think we are not supposed to. We survey our fantasy life and sometimes feel ashamed of the pictures that flash across the screen of our imagination.

We think that no one else in the human race or, perhaps, in all of history, has ever felt these emotional possibilities. And yet, our impulses and fantasies are not signs of depravity. They are instead lively signals of our humanity. How crushing it is to feel guilty about being human! Of themselves, these varied feelings are not indictable offenses. The more we can accept the many aspects of our humanity, the less troubled we are by them, and the more surely we will feel a sense of self-control and self-confidence. We are not strange just because we can have what seem to be strange thoughts and feelings.

potential

At times, however, it is not such seemingly shameful things that disturb us. We learn to deal with these things. We know that we are not going to act on all our impulses and that our fantasies do not represent reality. We learn that we are not all bad.

It is much harder for us to deal with what is good about ourselves—our talents and possibilities. One only has to be afraid to worry about fantasies. But one has to be alive to come to terms with goodness.

Sometimes we fight the pull of our own talents. We sense that if we commit ourselves to our possibilities, we will change, recognize an ability, let it see daylight, and we will have to grow. We may just become somebody different from who we are right now. We fear change because, no matter how much we dislike the present, at least it is familiar. But to commit ourselves to our possibilities! That is a journey of challenge where the end cannot be seen; it cannot even be guessed at.

What would we do with ourselves if we took our talents seriously, if we followed through on the unique combination of gifts that are ours? That very energy scares us; it seems too demanding, too mysterious. Thus we may fail to believe in ourselves because we do not want to believe in ourselves. We lack confidence not because it is denied us but because we refuse to accept it. And when we are afraid to do something, we can always find a thousand good reasons for not doing it.

fear of change

Closely related is our fear about expressing our true selves. Here risk looms like a mountain wall. It is dangerous to start climbing it because, once started, there is no coming down again. And we may get only dizzier as we go higher. We may shy away from what we really can do because this demands from us such a dangerous involvement with life. We know how much it hurts to be put down by other people, to be criticized for our best efforts, or to be laughed at when we are sincere. Is there anything more painful than to be told that we are silly or not yet grown up—or that we are out of fashion or out of step? The danger of ridicule is a strong deterrent to trusting our abilities and bringing them more fully into the light.

We develop a style to obscure what is best about us. We use strategies of delay and hesitation to keep our personalities unfinished and shapeless. Or we may use sarcasm or make light of everything to keep people

**How empty
is life
when it is reduced to
all the 'gusto'
you are supposed to
be able to grab
from
a can of beer.**

away from us. There are games galore that we not only learn to play but play expertly to protect ourselves from being too closely inspected by those around us.

With such defenses, we feel more secure. But these defenses may prevent the kind of exchange with others that we need for fuller growth. If we do not let others in, we cannot let the truth about ourselves out. We lock our possibilities in a darkened room because the sunlight looks dangerous. But, like most living things, we all need that sunlight to grow. It helps—even though it seems to hurt —to realize that we remain as we are because we want it that way. For reasons we may not want to admit, staying the way we are may be painful but is also the path of least resistance. We settle for an adjustment that does not really make us happy but which makes us less vulnerable to life. In other words, it may be less painful not to believe in ourselves than to believe in ourselves.

subjects, not objects

By treating ourselves this way, we make ourselves objects, not subjects in life. We observe ourselves as though from a distance, watching ourselves on a stage and prompting behavior that gets the applause of the audience. We may raise vigorous protests at being treated like objects by others, but frequently we handle ourselves in the same way. We literally push ourselves around, forcing ourselves into roles that do not match us.

Taking ourselves seriously does not mean taking ourselves solemnly. It means that we can approach ourselves with a respect for our own existence *despite our defects*. Indeed, the capacity to smile at our foibles—and sometimes to laugh uproariously at them—is one of the most liberating experiences that life can offer. That means that we take ourselves seriously enough to refuse to take ourselves solemnly. Few things are as healthy as refusing to try to impress either ourselves or others with our importance. When we can at least smile at ourselves, we find it easier to live with ourselves—and make it easier for others too.

How can we treat ourselves as subjects? We do it when we can speak an *I* about our experiences and feel the fullness of ourselves. Then we know we are in touch with what is true of us, and live in and through that. It is simple and difficult at the same time because it demands that we begin to live in the first person.

Perhaps we can only approach this by recognizing how often we live in the third person. By so doing we stand at a distance from ourselves. Instead of saying, "I trust my good instincts about this," we substitute "A good person does this or that in this situation." Our stage directions come from outside of us, from an external imperative that presses duty rather than free choice on us. If we can speak and live our lives in the first person we do not neglect duty, but we base our judgments on what is really going on inside ourselves. We are present as ourselves in life.

It is not such a difficult thing to do. We find that we feel better if we feel and speak for ourselves. We also discover that instead of rejecting us, people pay more positive attention to us. As we succeed this way, we become more comfortable with ourselves. We live as subjects and discover that others respect us as individuals. Just a small dose of self-confidence can free us from the prison of being an object in our own eyes. There is only one requirement: we have to think and speak our true convictions even if they are less than world-shaking in their impact. If they represent our own view, they are good enough.

Thus we know our powers as well as our limitations. When we live this way, we give ourselves room enough to come alive. We are not afraid to take responsibility for our own identity and actions. Such behavior is not the outcome of pride; it arises from the right kind of self love, the kind that makes room for everything that is real about us. We can live in the first person only if we are ready to take some of the risks that go with letting out the real truth about ourselves.

taking risks

Taking risks is the key to entering life more deeply, experiencing it in a happier and fuller fashion. When we no longer hide the truth about ourselves, others can see us truly, perhaps for the first time. We hear that recognition in the things people say when they glimpse something of each other's true personality. "You're not like everybody else," friends and lovers say to each other, "You're different." That is the kind of affirmation that comes to us when we give ourselves a chance at life.

Taking the risk of letting out the truth of ourselves makes that truth available to others. They respond immediately and positively. What attracts people is not what we pretend to be but what we are. They can see and understand the truth even though the truth is that we are imperfect, but they can only be confused when we manipulate or pretend our way through existence. Sometimes we are lonely and unsure of ourselves because we never give others even a glance at what we are really like. It is not that they do not want to see. It is rather that we are unwilling to reveal the truth. It is not that they are unwilling to draw close; it is that we keep them at a distance. These are obstacles that we ourselves control, that we can do something about. We can start taking a look at what we have so long been hiding about ourselves. That is a big act of trust in ourselves, beginning of greater belief in our own truth. It is a big step toward a deeper sense of self-confidence.

CHAPTER THREE

What is There to Like in Me?

That is another common question that we usually do not ask out loud. It is the kind we whisper to ourselves, somewhat uncertainly, and with some degree of wistfulness. "What could anybody see in me?" echoes in a thousand hearts—perhaps in our own—this very moment.

When we are asked to describe ourselves, we usually do not sound like press agents introducing a superstar. "I am a very ordinary person," we say, "Nothing special really. . ." That is the way we look at ourselves. It is not, of course, the way we always want other people to look at us. We want to be special to somebody else. We want it so much that we can die as human beings from the lack of it.

As much as we need food and water, just that much and more, we need someone to like us just as we are, to single us out and to treat us as individuals, not as just a part of the general crowd. There is nothing wrong with needing and wanting someone to like us in a unique way. We get into trouble only when we do not like ourselves and as a result make mistakes trying to force others to like us; that is different from letting them like us just as we are.

Sometimes, for example, we pick out the people we would like to have pick us out. We are highly selective. We like to impress the people who impress us and so we construct strategies—some of them as old as the dropped handkerchief or the carefully arranged "accidental" meeting. But how often these carefully outfitted expeditions that hunt for affection are outwitted by their quarry. The big ones always seem to get away. And we are left wondering whatever happened to us.

How crushing it is when we fail to gain the attention of somebody we want to notice us. Is there anything harder on the human heart than being ignored by the very person whose response we desperately long for? Then, as

There is nothing wrong with needing and wanting someone to like us in a unique way.

we look back, we feel awkward and ashamed at the way we may have thrown ourselves at somebody else. Often we do not even like to think about these episodes. Even the common phrases we use in these circumstances catch some of the regret that we feel in retrospect. "I made a fool of myself," we will say or, "I did things that made me look ridiculous." Obviously, we are not very proud of some of these campaigns for affection. As a result we feel still less confident about our own like-ableness.

The funny thing is that many of the best things in life actually happen by accident. The greatest plans fall apart when people use too much cunning in trying to trap happiness. Happiness approaches us sideways, catching us when we are not even looking in its direction, surprising us when we are able to forget ourselves. So it is with love, with that wondrous experience we know when somebody else looks at us in a special way and sees who we are just in ourselves.

ourselves as others see us

A lover looks at us from a different angle than the one we use to look at ourselves. Somebody else views us from the side and can suddenly say or do something that reaches us, that touches what is true in us and makes us feel more alive. Often enough this is not the person whose attention we are working so hard to get. We are surprised and perhaps even a little confused when somebody sees us as we are when we had not realized they were looking in our direction. Somebody likes us when we are not even trying to win their affection. Somebody likes us, not because we are trying to impress them, but because he or she can see more of us than we can see of ourselves. Such people cast a vote in favor of the things we have ignored in ourselves; they give us a new view of ourselves and a new way to believe in who we are.

What is it that such persons see? And why is it that we fail to see it even when we are desperately anxious to get someone else's attention? What is there of worth that this other person is able to see about us at the very moment when we are working hard to be somebody else? How can we get a better look at what they see? And how do we then get in touch with this truth and develop a good, comfortable relationship with this part of ourselves? Where and how do we begin?

the self of our experience

We start with our own human experience. Where else could we start? If we begin with fancy or imagination, we are already far outside of our own reality. If we start by trying to pretend to be something we are not, we make it harder to see who we are. But our experience tells us who we are. This is not the experience we call the best teacher. It is something else, the very fabric of our days, the raw material out of which we fashion our lives. This experience refers to the things that go on inside us in relation to the things that go on outside us. Such experience has to do with our emotions, those litmus-paper reactions that tell us so much about our own personalities. And this experience includes what others feel toward us and how this shapes the way we feel toward ourselves. Experience is the stuff of our own autobiography, the bedrock truth about who we are, where we have been, and what it means to us.

Some theorists say that there are really two levels of personality. There is, first of all, the person we really are. This is the person of experience, the self made up of

**Experience
is the stuff of our own
autobiography,
the bedrock truth
about
who we are,
where we have been,
and what it means
to us.**

what really happens to us, the truth that cannot be contradicted or wished away. These elemental factors—love, hate, confusion, and a hundred other things—are the building blocks of our existence. We are loved, cared for, forgotten at times, left alone at others. Name any of the wide range of human adventures that form us, and we have all tasted at least a small portion of each one of them. Think of our reactions: we are content, peaceful, loving; but we can also be afraid, jealous, angry, and sometimes just downright achingly miserable. These all become a part of ourselves; they are all in there someplace, in some combination. It is this experience that tells us what we are really like.

our view of ourselves

The other, second level of personality can be, but is not automatically, related to our self of genuine experience. This is the way we view ourselves, the picture we have of our personalities. Often this view of the self of experience is out of focus. Many factors affect our image of ourselves. We may not let ourselves see everything that is there in our experience. We may misinterpret some of it or misname parts of it. Our picture of ourselves, in other words, depends on what we permit ourselves to see, as well as on the names we give to what we experience.

Our picture of ourselves—our self-image as some call it—can be accurate, as candid as a news photo, but it can also be dimly lit and full of the soft shadows used by photographers to mask the wrinkles in aging glamour girls. We cannot clearly see the things that are in those heavy shadows. It is hard sometimes even to guess at what they might be. We keep ourselves from seeing our freckles, lines, or any of the other telltale signs of our human situation. If we keep ourselves enough out of focus psychologically we cannot even sense what we feel like. We may look more like we were carved out of ivory than composed of flesh and blood. If we do not examine or name the feelings in our experience correctly, we can be very unsure of who we are.

In extreme cases we refuse to look at any picture of ourselves at all. We indulge rather in our own science-fiction, sketching an ideal version of ourselves and attempting to live by it even when it does not at all resemble us. This is a way of living by something in our mind's eye that is never in our real eye. It is living by a fantasy that only we perceive. We live not in touch with our real experience but with what we imagine it to be.

distorting the image

This self-picture gets us into trouble when it does not match the self of our experience. When that happens—when we do not fit together psychologically—we lack the protection of a secure identity. Exposed on all sides, we are constantly vulnerable. So it becomes doubly difficult to see ourselves or to feel very comfortable when our notions of ourselves are distorted or unreal. We find it almost impossible to feel very good about ourselves, and others receive confusing messages from us. This in turn put us further on edge, increasing our fear that at some level people will see through us. The tension involved in trying to keep up appearances can exhaust us when we are not sure of who we are underneath.

Exploring some examples of how these two selves—the real one of experience and the self-picture—conflict can make this process clearer to us. In the self of real experience we may be angry. In our picture of ourselves, however, we may be convinced that we never get angry. We do not admit this feeling because it is inconsistent with our idea of ourselves. Have you ever heard somebody say "I am not angry!" in a loud and angry voice? There are two messages there, the real anger, and the effort to deny the anger. That is the confusion many of us live with and communicate to others constantly.

Or take the possibility that we are lazy and are not working very hard on some project in the office or at school. In our picture of ourselves we may feel that we are very hard working. We may even protest that we are tired from toiling so diligently at our tasks. There is a big discrepancy here, but who sees the truth? Our companions or colleagues can see clearly enough that we are not working hard. But can we see it when we are trying so hard to convince ourselves that the opposite is really true of us? That is when we must live behind psychological defenses.

Suppose that in the self of real experience we are average looking with, as most of us have, some attractive qualities. In our mind's eye, however, we may not think we are good looking at all and we may deny or not be able to see our best qualities. And we act on that distorted picture of ourselves, looking away from what is positive about us. But other people see us as we are. They may smile compassionately when we refuse to accept what they can see of our attractiveness. We keep looking away, unwilling to look at who we are. Thus living by an untrue image of ourselves not only throws us out of balance but affects all our relationships with others.

Or we may be genuinely tender. In our self-image, however, we may reject tenderness because of some immature idea that we demonstrate strength by acting tough or harsh. Frequently people hide good qualities precisely because they mistakenly feel they should be ashamed of them. It may be that in the real world we are likeable persons. In our way of looking at ourselves, however, we may feel so guilty that we cannot believe that anybody else could like us.

Everybody has good qualities: a friendly smile, an engaging laugh, clear and honest eyes. There are inner qualities we need to see as well. In the self of real experience, for example, we may be bright and sensitive. In our picture of ourselves, however, we may deny this or water these qualities down so that we can describe ourselves as "just ordinary." We hold back using these strengths, hiding them under a false interpretation of ourselves, keeping at a distance from what we are really like and making it harder for others to approach us at the same time. We are, in the deepest sense, defending against our own possibilities as persons.

aligning our experience with our image

Whenever these worlds—that of true experience and that of our picture of ourselves—are far apart, we become uncomfortable with ourselves and unsure of how we will react. Our relationship to ourselves —and therefore our sense of self-worth— depends on getting these two worlds lined up with each other. When the self of our true experience and our self-picture match each other, we are in a state of good adjustment. What we truly are in experience is matched by our accurate perception of that experience. There is no looking away, no search for disguises, and no misnaming of what happens to us either inside or out. These worlds coincide when we recognize our feelings and give them their right names, whether we are experiencing anger or tenderness. We live in the real world when we live with our real selves. We fit together when we can call a spade a spade about our psychological reactions. The heart of keeping ourselves— literally these two selves—together lies in naming our experience correctly.

Our experience always needs proper labeling. Sometimes we have to reexamine and relabel things that we have had wrong before. "No, I guess I'm not that way after all," we say as we revise our notion of ourselves in a more honest direction. Most of us can, in fact, make an honest appraisal of ourselves. We can surrender the defensive distortions that may limit our notions of ourselves. We can discover a more trustworthy self and begin to live in and through it. We then feel a new wholeness about ourselves. We can believe in ourselves, and this, of course, makes it easier for others to believe in us as well.

Most of us discover the truth about our experience if we just stop to listen to ourselves a little more carefully and patiently. We can find the right names for what we experience whether it is joy or loneliness. We feel better when we label our experience more accurately even when it is a difficult or disappointing experience. There are no better friends than those who let us explore our feelings at our own pace and who do not push us too fast or too far with notions of their own. Those who love us let us find our own way; they help by not forcing us to distort our picture of ourselves. Sometimes they give us the words we need when we cannot find them for ourselves. But once we find the right description of what we experience we can put that in our self-picture by ourselves. And each time we do that we feel better and surer about who we are.

the truth frees us for growth

Finding the truth allows us to come to terms with who we really are. It does not, however, mean that we need to be content with our faults. When we have a clear view of our faults, we can begin to do something sensible and constructive to correct them. We can grow out of them instead of covering them up the way we throw a shawl over a worn out chair. We can give up defenses by getting a better view of what needs developing in ourselves. We give them up because we do not need them when we have learned to be honest with ourselves. A great sense of relief comes when we no longer have to cover over our faults or strengths. We can just be who we are.

The first step involves shifting our angle of vision. Maybe we have to come, like those surprising strangers, from the side in order to see the truth we would not let ourselves see head on. We can then make our way homeward to our true self, the self we can count on because it is solid and real. But the way there depends on getting these aspects of our personality together. What goes on in our experience must be matched by an accurate label for it in our picture of ourselves. This is a constant process because we are always having new experiences. But once we get a sense of how to do it, we can be much more at ease with ourselves. We know who we are and can let the truth show to others. We may be pleasantly surprised to find how much there is to like in ourselves.

CHAPTER FOUR

Hearing Ourselves

Getting a more accurate picture of ourselves is the beginning of believing more in ourselves. But we need not only a clear picture but a sound track of ourselves. Then we can begin to hear as well as see ourselves as we really are. Again, our best resource—and one often neglected—is ourselves. All too often when we want to find out about ourselves, we ask somebody else. How strange it is, when we consider the amount of time we can spend talking about ourselves. For many of us, that means every chance we can get. Yet it comes as a surprise when it is suggested that we begin to seek self-knowledge by looking at and listening to, not experts, but ourselves.

The fact is that we are always talking and much of it is about ourselves. Much of what we say about ourselves, however, is indirect. We may in some instances have to "overhear" ourselves, but the evidence is usually there if we take the time to listen and observe carefully. We are always giving signals about ourselves in what we do and in what we say. We are always making marks so that we can follow the trail to the truth about ourselves more easily.

But listening to ourselves—like telling the truth for some politicians—seems like either the last resort or a secret weapon. That is not surprising especially if we don't believe in ourselves. Then we pay very little attention to what we say or do. We may miss much of our real experience because we do not appreciate the significance of what we say or do. Not that we are hiding things deliberately on ourselves; we are always giving out truthful information. But if we do not believe in ourselves to begin with, we will not believe or pay much attention to what we say about ourselves.

living or killing our lives

Suppose we pause for a moment to observe the way we spend each day. Sometimes we

We are always giving signals about ourselves in what we do and in what we say.

do not spend the day as much as kill it by slowly strangling it to death. Sometimes we live in constant wait for something that is supposed to happen after we finish whatever it is that we are actually doing, whether it is school work, our job, or simply a conversation. And when we do get through, we are often not quite able to remember what it was that we were so anxious to do. Then evening comes, we take off our shoes and are alone at last. We have survived the day. But what does that mean if we live holding ourselves back from our work or from our play, always waiting for something else to happen?

At other times we may spend our day as a series of little bridges leading from one minor occasion to another. We may, for example, wait for breakfast to be served and then we may wait for the news to come on radio or television. After that we can wait for the paper and after that comes the wait for the mail. We can also wait for a coffee break or for lunch, for the ballgame to begin, the evening news, dinner and, at last, we wait for that familiar outpost for many Americans, the final weather forecast of the day. Why? We are not going anyplace. And, if we are not careful, we will spend tomorrow the same way. We manage to get through the hours that way like someone climbing hand over hand up a long ladder. But it is a dulling experience and we end up unsure of where we have been or where we are going. We can easily miss ourselves and our lives in the process.

tuning in to ourselves

But there are other patterns to observe and ours may be a fresh one, more informative than we might have supposed. What we talk about, the things we do, the priorities we set —all these reflect our beliefs and our values. Through these we write our signature on life. Such occurrences in our experience tell us who we are. What are some of the specific areas to which we might turn our eyes and our ears in pursuit of our real selves?

How do we listen to people? What attitudes do we manifest in the way we receive and make room for others in our lives? The way we deal with others tells us quite clearly about our characteristic way of dealing with ourselves. Our style with others is merely a reflection of our style with ourselves. Hence it is a good place to begin our quest.

Do we find ourselves always judging others, sorting them out as good or bad, interesting or dull, according to our own whims or inclinations? Or do we perceive others as at least mildly threatening, as though they are all likely to become competitors with us for some vague or distant prize? Are we edgy about our privacy and do we use strategies to keep people at a distance or on the very borders of our lives? Do we look at people as persons with rights and lives of their own or do we perceive them as problems to us that have to be handled? Sometimes we complain about being lonely but, as we watch ourselves dealing with other persons, we may discover that we have a big hand in maintaining our own isolation.

the pecking order of our lives

What do we do first? This reveals our priorities. It tells us what we believe in because the activities we put first ride point on the rest of the day's business. What comes first tells us symbolically what we count as most significant in our picture of ourselves. It tells us something about our needs. We may be tempted to deny the truth that comes out. But

**Sometimes
we do not spend
the day
so much as kill it
by slowly
strangling it
to death.**

there is the evidence and we cannot completely look away from it. Whatever gets our first
attention and our first energies says something about us quite distinctly.

What do we do last? This defines the
lower bracket of our set of values, the things
that can be postponed or that we do not feel
much like doing, the things we value least of
all. These are not necessarily minor activities.
But whatever their size, when we push them
to the edge of our lives, we are saying something about ourselves.

What are the things we never quite get
done at all? These are easy to find because
we can hear ourselves saying, ''I've been
meaning to get around to that,'' or ''I'm,
going to do something about this some day.''
We may not have to look very far or very
deeply to find out why we do postpone
things. We can recognize that we strive to
avoid potential conflicts, or dealing with certain persons, or that we delay straightening
out certain aspects of our own lives. We do
these things to ourselves. The things that do
not get done are that way because we want
them that way. We are not victims in this
situation and, if we are honest, we can begin
to dig deeper to understand better why we
behave in this way.

What are the things for which we would make sacrifices? What, in other words, are the activities for which we would give up sleep, time, or privacy to accomplish? These also help tell us what we are like. We all know there are certain things that are never too much trouble for us to do. Then there is a whole other class of things that are always too much trouble to do. Somewhere in the contrast between those categories there is a big truth about the self of our real experience.

making others pay

Who do we let pay for our own lateness or delays? Who is the scapegoat in our lives? We can find the answer to this question in the pattern of the way we handle the events of our lives. We may discover that, although it is our own poor planning or lack of attention that gets us into certain scrapes, we always expect somebody else to pay our way out. There is, for example, the person whose rights we are ready to step on because we know that we can get away with it. There may be those whose appointments are the first ones we cancel if an emergency arrives.

There may be persons we are ready to inconvenience because we feel that we can get away with it at the least emotional cost to ourselves. If we think about it—let ourselves see ourselves in action—and the ones we inconvenience always turn out to be the same persons in our lives, we have learned something about our style, and something very important about our truth.

what others see

All these bring us back to the question of how we see ourselves. Are we in focus, in the shadows, or have we captured a fairly good likeness? The accuracy of our self-picture depends on whether we do listen to or watch ourselves in our dealings with other persons. The Scottish poet Robert Burns wrote of the great gift we would have if we could see ourselves as others see us. But that is hard, and we may give up too easily.

I am reminded of an old friend with whom I had dinner a few years ago. I had not seen him in some time, and when he arrived, I noticed his appearance had been notably changed by the jet black wig he was wearing. He seemed calm and self-assured, but my eyes were drawn to it. I could not help myself even with the mightiest of efforts. I was like one hypnotized gazing back at this new acquisition. We sat at dinner and, although I tried to look out a window, at other people in the restaurant, or at the sugar bowl, my eyes kept fixing directly on the new wig that lay on his head about as subtly as a dead deer on the front of a hunter's car.

In the middle of the meal, my friend leaned forward and said quietly, "I have a secret to tell you. . . ." At this my giggles erupted. I had to bite my napkin as, with no idea of how he was being perceived, he went on to tell me that his hair was not his own. I felt embarassed at not being able to restrain my laughter, but he did not seem to notice at all. He went on talking, obviously proud of his own picture of himself, but without a clue as to how the world saw him.

I have often thought since then that we must all have behaviors and quirks that stand out just as clearly as that man's wig and that we can go along just as serenely self-deluded, our own truth clear to everybody but ourselves. It is not easy to see ourselves, but it would be a complete tragedy to miss even a passing glance at what we are really like as we lead our lives. That takes patience, a willingness to listen, and almost always a willingness to laugh at ourselves.

the message of our feelings

This is not necessarily a ruthless or difficult business. Sometimes it sounds too painful to listen. But what would we hear, say, if we listened as carefully as we could just to our feelings? We talk to ourselves through our feelings all the time. When we fit together pretty well as persons, our feelings help interpret life to us. They pass judgment on people and events. They tell us what we like and what we are afraid of and, perhaps, some things that we have a right to be suspicious of. Listening to our feelings is not tuning in on a bad program. It is rather a way of hearing ourself first hand, of getting vital information about who we are. It is a way of tapping into the truth in the self of our experience.

The best part about our feelings is that they are a source not of rumors but of accurate information about ourselves. They can be quite trustworthy. We can count on them as guides in life when we are honest and label them correctly. When we say that we can count on our feelings, we are also saying that we can learn to count on ourselves. We are, in a very real sense, our own best friends. But we have to listen to hear what we have to say to ourselves. This is a way of treating our own personality with respect, of getting in touch with the truth we can build our lives on.

As we listen carefully, we begin to note the things that can threaten us and bring our defenses into play. When we are patient and can get to the bottom of these, we become more comfortable with our truth and learn to live with it. We no longer need to erect elaborate defenses. We no longer need to insist that we are somebody we really are not.

When we do not need our defenses quite so much anymore, we do not have to look outside ourselves for things to prop up our self-esteem. We will not manipulate or use others to make ourselves feel better. We will, in a simple phrase, know the difference between ourselves and others. Knowing that —and respecting that in life—deepens our self-esteem and gives us a chance for real love from somebody else.

self-esteem must come from within

If we do not listen to ourselves, we do not believe in ourselves from the inside. Then we can spend our lives searching for something outside us to provide the self-confidence we need to solve our problems. We need the proofs of self-esteem to come from outside of ourselves and we may manifest this in a dozen different ways. Many childhood disturbances, for example, are indications of the search for self-esteem. Many children speak a special emotional language with a simple and familiar message. They want and need the attention of somebody else.

It is also true that some adolescents, despite what they tell themselves, are not really looking for love in their search for the right girl or boy. They are looking for someone to prop up their self-esteem. They feel that being married may do this for them. What they marry is usually just an extension of themselves, some fantasy projected on the other. Then in the reality of marriage they discover that the other person is not at all what they expected. How sad the words recited in so many divorce petitions: two people did not really know each other and got married anyway. They did not know

**Listening
to our feelings
is a way of
getting
vital information
about
who we are.**

their true selves of experience. They thought they married for an experience they called love, but in truth it was to bolster their self-esteem that they married.

Persons can use many unfortunate routes to the goal of self-esteem. Peer pressure is enormous for young people and so to secure acceptance or the approval of the group, they may involve themselves in drinking, drugs, or sexual relations. All of these activities, no matter how they are rationalized or celebrated, may be used to boost their self-esteem. They do not become confident adults through these things; they make that a more difficult goal for themselves all the time.

Much damage can be done, in other words, in this quest for self-esteem, especially when young people are blinded to the real nature of what they are looking for, when they do not know how to label their own experience. But there is a road that is sure and only seems more difficult than others. It opens to those who can stand aside from the pressures of the crowd in a quiet place and there listen to themselves and hear what is really going on. There they can get in touch with and finally trust their own feelings, and find their way confidently and truthfully through life. That is the only way home for any of us.

CHAPTER FIVE

Being Our Own Best Friend

Melville Cane, a poet-lawyer in his nineties, was once asked the secret of his long life. When he was sure that his questioner was serious, he answered, "I've lived with my pain." Only a person who has learned to be a friend to himself could say that. Such persons thrive not by vainly congratulating themselves on their goodness, their looks, or even their accomplishments. They live fully by being human with themselves, by facing the inevitability of pain in any purposeful life, and by making peace with all that is true about themselves. Such persons take themselves seriously but not solemnly; their self-picture matches their self of experience.

That is an important lesson for us if we wish to believe more in ourselves. The pain of being alive is not something we treat with a new wonder drug. Life is not an illness for which we must seek a cure. We do not act as though we were afflicted by existence and needed a miracle to escape it. We just live it as truly as we can, in touch with our truth as honestly as we can be. That is the basis for our being friendly with ourselves.

Now it is true that we cannot do much about some of the sufferings life hands to us except to face them. But there are other pains about which we can do something. There is unnecessary suffering, for example, in our lives if we feel uncomfortable because we are not perfect human beings. We feel at least vaguely guilty because we cannot rid ourselves of shortcomings. We then feel unhappy because we are still basically unfinished. We are sad, in other words, about an essential characteristic of our human nature. It is like a bird mourning the capacity to fly. Or, in another mood, despising our gift of laughter. When we do not like what is so basic to our condition we introduce a great deal of superfluous suffering into our lives. We refuse to grant ourselves permission to be human.

**Life
is not an
illness
for which
we must seek
a cure.**

just being human

Much of our pain and uncertainty lifts away, however, when we can welcome ourselves into the human race. A deep kind of peace—the kind nobody can take away from us—settles on us when we come to terms with our humanity, when we are content that we still have some growing to do. That is an indispensable lesson in learning to like ourselves like good friends.

We would be hard pressed, after all, to prove that we are the greatest of sinners. It seems perfectly safe to allow us on the street even after dark. Neither adults nor children are threatened by our presence in society. Search ourselves as we might we probably could not really impress anybody with a list of our sins or short comings. We might even find many good things that recommend us as having some worth after all. The only wanted list most of us are on is the one we tack up for ourselves when we refuse to accept the fact that we are still composed of loose ends and imperfections. Who accuses us? We do, most of the time. And the bill of particulars? Vague and undocumented.

Giving ourselves a ticket of admission to the human family relieves us of trying to exist like pure spirits or those Hollywood heroes who never muss their hair or run out of ammunition. Despite the paralyzing new hair sprays, hardly any of us survives a day with every hair in place. We are lucky to get through life with our own hair or teeth, for that matter. And we regularly run out of energy, time, and sometimes even good humor. But that does not make us bad or unlovable; it just makes us human.

healing laughter

It is here, of course, that laughter can cure us. Stand off a little from ourselves and we can look more gently at our shortcomings and even smile at our minor vanities. Laughing gently at ourselves forgives us for our failings and heals us of our wounds. Laughter is not solemn, but it is wonderfully serious because it can support the weight of our lives. Laughter protects us from that stifling solemnity that brings us down like a mantle of cement. Friendly laughter deflates us, but it does not kick the wind out of us. It offers a suddenly more open and accepting attitude to ourselves. It says, in effect, come, join the rest of us in the human race, the amusing family to which you belong.

This is a big step because, as we live more comfortably with our humanity, we obtain the strength to live with any pain that comes our way. We have a way of understanding and handling our suffering, of seeing it as something less than the end of the world, as something we can, with a better sense of who we are, manage quite well.

doers not victims

But we can only do this if we meet the challenges of life actively rather than passively. Life is not a plague that is somehow unjustly inflicted on us. It is not something that just happens to us; we are not victims of existence. If we feel that way—as though we were inmates in a psychological jail—it is because we pull the barred door shut from the inside. We may feel locked in, but we hold the keys in our own hands. So, after accepting ourselves, the next step toward becoming more friendly to—and more confident in—ourselves lies in taking positive responsibility for the shape of our own existence.

If we seem to be sitting out the action of life in the penalty box, we should ask ourselves: What am I getting out of this anyway? Why do I let myself get sidetracked? What reward is in it? Why should I choose something for myself that makes me feel miserable?

Only we can answer these direct questions. And half the time we remain miserable only because we do not ask them. We remain in a punishing situation only if there is some reward for us in staying there. We do not remain hesitant and unsure about our own worth unless we feel more comfortable being tentative rather than confident about ourselves. Why would we ever be that way? Well there are some dubious rewards in remaining uncommitted about ourselves. Keep your opinions open, we are told, and you never have to embark on a journey where you will have to follow through. Don't choose and you will never have to test your worth in the fire. Only we can find the answers to explain our holding back from being ourselves.

There are other feelings involved in this. They are the emotions of persons standing in the cold looking in at the diners around the cozy fire. We can look in at life as wistfully as orphans in a Dickens story. The feast is always attractive, but we still hold ourselves aloof from it. If we find ourselves in this position, we should not curse our fate or feel sorry for ourselves. We can ask ourselves: why? Perhaps we are punishing ourselves, or keeping ourselves off balance, or we may be fearful that if we enjoy life a little bit, it will all be taken away from us. Better to hold back, then, and deny ourselves what we fear losing in the long run.

the enemy is fear

Fear about ourselves—and about the potential losses that would destroy our self-esteem—leads us to hide, to take the safe but ultimately shrivelling course of non-participation. That is the fear that causes us to hide. When we remain passively fearful, the dangers in life retain their power over us. We cringe in discomfort and try to stay as far away from them as possible. But the right kind of love for ourselves sets us free. When we love ourselves enough, we gain power over life's dangers. We take away their fear-someness; we triumph over them because our power to love is greater than theirs to destroy.

what might have been

Letting fear get the best of us can have tragic results. There may be nothing sadder than people who spend their lives talking about what they might have been. The woods are full of older men, for example, who still nourish themselves on the thin gruel of athletic careers they never pursued. How many times have you heard somebody say, "I had a chance to try out with the Yankees"? Sadder still are those who say "I could have gone to medical school. . ." or "I could have been an actress. . ." They are all using words of the Marlon Brando character of the boxer in the movie "On The Waterfront," who said to his brother, "I could have been a contender."

We are always safe in saying these things after the fact, after the chance has not been taken, after the fear that destroys self-confidence and self-esteem triumphs over us. That, however, is no way for anybody to grow old or even middle-aged. It is certainly no way to be young. Not when we can actively do something about it by facing ourselves truthfully in the present. We do not have to be victims in life. When we play that role we are ready to let opportunities for education, business success, or even love, slip by. Then we can only remember possibilities which for some reason we never faced, we denied to ourselves. We are victims in life when we want to be.

on the bench of life

We then resemble those athletes who get themselves put on the inactive list because that is just where they want to be. It is an effort to preserve self-esteem by not risking their talents in a real contest. Their possibilities are never tested. They never know whether they would be good or not. But, of course, they have a wonderful excuse, a minor injury, a bit of bad luck.

How similar we can sound! Fate is just against us, we say. It could happen to anyone. Or is it really that we are against ourselves? Did we make it happen? When we do not believe in ourselves, we are already the biggest obstacle in our own paths. Although we may find some good reason to explain what has happened to us, we are the true authors of that "unjust" fate. But this approach prevents us from ever finding out

who we are, and what we might be, and how deeply we might love and be loved.

friends with ourselves

Does this happen? And what, if we genuinely want to be more friendly to ourselves, can we do about it? We begin by realizing that friendship with ourselves is not modeled on a coach-player relationship. We are not trying to talk or shame ourselves—or in any other way manipulate ourselves—into more daring activities. Recklessness in the name of vanity is no way to demonstrate love for ourselves. Friendship with ourselves is not based on the salesman-client model either. We cannot sell ourselves to ourselves and expect it to work.

Real friendship with ourselves is built on a truthful recognition of our own existence; it flows from our readiness to respond to ourselves. We must allow ourselves to emerge. We have to learn to wait for ourselves, to listen to the inner voice that expresses who we are.

listening to ourselves

Pause to listen and what would we hear? We would hear the messages of our feelings, the very messages we so often ignore or to which we pay little attention. There is so much noise in life that they are sometimes drowned out. And we are often in such a hurry to do this or that that we do not listen at all. These messages are always there, however, and all we need is some time and a quiet place in which to listen to them.

I recently asked a cross-section of college students to take the time to listen to themselves and to write a brief description of what they heard. The following messages were received:

Over the weekend I had an experience with a friend of mine that caused me to examine our friendship and listen to my feelings about our relationship.

After this experience, I found that I was really frustrated in the relationship. I realized this exchange was characteristic of our whole relationship.

I found that I had ambivalent feelings. I wanted to just break off the relationship and not give any more of myself—not put myself out or work at the relationship anymore, yet I didn't want to lose the relationship. When I really thought out these feelings, I found that I wanted to save the relationship and make it better more than

I wanted to give it up. After I made this decision, I felt relieved and happy that I had made a decision.

I met a friend I had not seen for a while, and we began to talk. All he seemed to have on his mind was sports, which disappointed me since I was more curious about his current state of mind, which I couldn't believe was limited to athletics. I was aware of my own efforts to move the conversation in this other direction, but he kept coming back to games and scoring averages. In the past we had spent hours on this subject, but with my interest here waning and new interests rising, I suddenly realized that my old friend and I were parting ways, if we had not already split. In a sense he was serving notice that we were growing apart, although I really don't believe that he was aware of it. It occurred to me that this growing apart had been going on for some time and that it was no accident that we had not seen each other for some time, but that only now was I fully, consciously aware of it. Once I had comprehended this, I no longer tried to steer the conversation toward anything

We are
victims
in life
when we
want to be.

more personal. In effect I was waving my friend goodbye.

Since I spend most of my free time with my boyfriend, and I can lie to myself most at these times, I listened to what I was saying to myself when I was with him.

Experience this other person, and let him experience me as I am. It's funny how he doesn't even have to use words to convey what he feels inside about life, himself, and me. I wish that I could be as sure of me as he is of himself. There is no place I'd rather be than here with Tom. When I experience the beauty of him, it makes me feel so alive, happy, and peaceful inside. I see him for the beautiful person he is, and wonder how I missed experiencing this for so long. I wish that I could always be with him. I wish that I could come to a truer understanding of myself so that I could be more of a person for Tom and for myself. We can make things work, because we've worked so hard to build our relationship to what it is now. It makes me very happy when we plan for the day we'll be married and the life we plan to continue building for ourselves. I feel so much love for him that I'm always thinking about him and me, and how much he means to me and my life. He has enabled me to grow as a person—to be me—to be whatever it is I want to be. And I have helped him to grow—each day I experience more of his inner beauty and I feel it all around me—and I thank God for the gift of this person.

I listened to myself when I was with my boyfriend. I have been going out with him for three years. This weekend he was really depressed because he is graduating from college this semester. He doesn't know what he wants to do with his life, where he wants to work.

I listened to myself when I was with him and what he was saying. I found I felt all the insecurity he did, what do we really mean to each other. Then I had to ask myself truthfully what it would be like without him. I know there would be a great empty spot, but could someone else fill it? This has been the first time we really talked about the two of us apart. The feeling inside was so great when we talked. I still don't know how we would function apart. I love him very much and I want to hold on to what we have together and both of us want to work to really fulfill ourselves together. It was really a beautiful experience inside to know that two people, us, will work together.

Before, I realized, we had both been taking the other for granted. It took time for some reflection to go on in myself. I felt much freer and closer at the same time. We are two separate people, together at the same time.

getting the message

In each case we find individuals listening to something that is already there in their experience. They are, by listening carefully, finding the right name or symbol for what is going on inside them. And in each case they recognize the validity of the message. They find that they can trust it and that it has genuine meaning for them. Through hearing their true selves they possess themselves more fully, they deepen their sense of their own trustworthiness, they feel more whole.

This is exactly what we can all do for ourselves. We can only do it, however, if we treat ourselves as whole persons. Many self-improvement courses or books treat us as though we could be put together in segments something like the Six Million Dollar Man. This week we will improve our memory and next week our will power. The week after that we can study some new sexual techniques and then next month we can learn how to win friends and influence people.

But we do not live in segments and we do not improve much by concentrating on only one aspect of ourselves. We are friendly to ourselves when we have some appreciation, not just for parts, but for the whole of ourselves. Looking at ourselves in this way makes it much easier to make enough room for the full truth of ourselves to emerge. What is needed for this? Nothing fancy or unfamiliar: we need patience, time, and understanding. Giving ourselves space and freedom makes it possible to grow from the inside.

It does not make much sense to try to talk ourselves into things that we do not feel, even when these are urged on us by popular fads or current tastes. We only hurt ourselves more when we try to convince ourselves that we feel one way when, down in the genuine self of experience, we actually feel quite the opposite. We cannot let anybody else talk us out of understanding what our true feelings are. Doing that we betray our own friendship with ourselves. Somebody, for example, who tries to talk a young woman into sexual relations before marriage may present her with all the supposedly sophisticated contemporary arguments. If down deep she does not feel right about this, she will hurt herself—even though the hurt may not show for a long time—by letting herself be talked into something that contradicts her own truth. Any person who cheats or finds good reasons to do less than a full day's work may be able to muffle or ignore inner feelings that brand this as wrong. But no matter what arguments such persons muster they fail themselves deeply. They neglect the truth of their experience and can no longer even hear themselves.

In the long run manipulation, false persuasion, being too political with ourselves all fail. They fail because they are addressed to something less than our human fullness. We are not present even to ourselves when we fail to take our own personalities seriously enough to treat ourselves with the respect that their wholeness deserves.

the miracle of growth

Our growth is a long, slow miracle. It does not happen overnight. It does not occur just because we spend a lot of energy, or offer ourselves false arguments about what will gain us popularity with the crowd. The miracles in life—and most of them have to do with growth—depend on changes that occur within rather than outside us. That is the way our capacity to be friendly and trusting in ourselves develops. It goes along with the emergence of what is right and true about our own personalities. This depends always on patience and understanding. We may spend all day chasing a butterfly and never catch it. But if we sit still for a moment it will come and light on our shoulder. This is the way growth in self-confidence takes place. It follows when we pause to hear and live our own truth.

In trying to force open a clam shell, a frustrated person may use a knife and end up cutting his own finger. He just grows angrier because he cannot open up the reluctant clam. The wonder is that if you put the clam in the warm sand and leave it alone it will open all by itself, from the inside. There is something to be learned from butterflies and clams. Our real self is there and, if we give it half a chance, it will emerge strong and true and all by itself.

CHAPTER SIX

Does It Hurt Too Much?

Well, you may say, it is all very well to talk about taking the risk of stepping more bravely into life. But being hurt is not just a risk, it is a sure thing in life. And that is what hurts so much. Knowing that hurt lies out there somewhere makes it hard to believe in oneself or to have much confidence that one can ever do better than just protect oneself from the bad things that may happen.

There is no sense in denying it. The world's streets are filled with the walking wounded, people who have been hurt by life and have never quite been the same again. They feel miserable about what has happened to them. They begin to wonder what is wrong with them, if they are really lovable at all. They did reach out, they say, only to be rejected. They tried to enter into life, just as everybody says one should, only to find that they were almost drowned in the quicksand of emotional involvement.

We have all tasted the confusion of pain that comes when we seek a share of life and a measure of love. That is what really hurts. "I tried it once," we say in a tone that is more mourning than celebration, "and I'll never let myself get that involved again." We draw back to be a little more careful the next time.

But can we write off the only opportunity to experience our fullness just because there are hazards along the way? When we are weary of hurt, that is just what we do. We want some distance between ourselves and others. There has been too much pain in getting close to others. We may not know exactly what happened and we may not even be able to make sense out of it now. But we do not want to take the chance of being hurt again. So we introduce safeguards against caring too much. We dig a moat to protect our injured self-esteem.

We may want to be more personal in our relationships, but we regretfully decide that we can only survive by making them less so. We want to save ourselves from losing both our heads and our hearts at the same time. A battered heart is hesitant to take love's risks again. We may spend our lives trying to recover the self-confidence we lost in a bad experience of excessive emotional involvement.

facing the risks

Can we learn something helpful here? Something that may save our self-esteem and make it less necessary to retreat? Can we face the possibilities of hurt without shrinking from life to avoid it? The answer, if we will allow ourselves to be human, is *yes*. We can indeed learn much about the tricky questions of emotional involvement. We can learn things about ourselves that enable us to avoid crushing and unnecessary pain as we seek to live more closely with others. We can love without destroying our self-confidence.

What is it like to be excessively emotionally involved? Every one of us has had some experience of this. Usually we find ourselves emotionally involved before we realize what is happening. Somebody may have warned us about it, but we were too young or inexperienced to understand exactly what they were talking about. All we know is that we responded to somebody else, that we opened ourselves to someone to whom we were attracted, we took a deep drink of the heady wine we thought was love, and the world fell in on us.

misguided involvement

This can happen when we are wide open, vulnerable in every way. We may have found that we became so concerned about somebody else that we could think of little else. We were concerned about the other's welfare all the time, had this person remembered to bring an umbrella on a rainy day, did this other person get the assignments that were important for this course, was the other person capable of existing without our assistance. Excessive emotional involvement centers on our investment of all our meaning in another person. And too often the relationship collapses doing great damage to our sense of ourselves. When our sense of worth—whether we feel lovable or not—depends on the response of some other person to us, we are off balance. We can do nothing but fall.

A
battered heart
is hesitant
to take
love's risks
again.

Sometimes when we fall this way, we lose any desire to get up again. We feel destroyed and wonder whether we could ever risk ourselves again in a relationship with another human being. We are like the young man in A.E. Houseman's poem who at twenty-one took no heed of the dangers of emotional involvement only to say later, "The heart out of the bosom was never given in vain; 'tis paid with sighs aplenty and sold for endless rue, and I am two and twenty and oh, 'tis true, 'tis true."

keeping ourselves whole

What can we do to preserve ourselves without selling ourselves out? How can we move forward in life without being ground up in the terrible machinery of excessive emotional involvement? This is where learning to listen to our real selves is vitally important. Indeed it is indispensable if we are to maintain our own separate identity and still remain able to share who we are generously with others. Hearing what is going on inside us enables us to maintain possession of ourselves so that we are less upset by having feelings that we never recognized within us before. Our ability to take the risks of the love that validates our self-worth depends on our awareness of all aspects of ourselves, our thorough acquaintance with our self of experience.

This is an operational way of being our own best friend. We do not stand around saying "You're wonderful" to ourselves. Rather, we do just what any good friend does for another. We try to be present to ourselves and to listen to what we are saying so that we can understand it. We have to hear ourselves in order to be ourselves. We run dangerous risks of excessive emotional involvement only when we are not listening to ourselves and do not understand what is taking place in our own personalities. We are vulnerable only when we are blind to what we are really like. Then we do not know what we have to give to somebody else. We do not know the measure of our involvement because we have lost the sense of ourselves along the way.

straight with ourselves, open with others

When we are aware of what is taking place in ourselves, when we face it and give it its right name, then we can be open with others without fear of betraying ourselves. We can be close to them and yet not lose ourselves completely in their emotional problems. We need not be torn apart by their conflicts nor so totally identified with them that we lose our own shape and end up like psychological protoplasm. We can still care at close range without being totally consumed or destroyed by our own passion. We can live deeply—and with a better sense of our own value—when we do not lose track of the self of our true experience.

The typically crushing emotional involvement occurs when we are victims of our own needs. We think we are reaching out to somebody else but are really responding to something within ourselves. We want to be wanted by this other. We want the recognition or the affection that the other seems to promise to us.

Sometimes we even try to secure our own identity by deriving it from someone else. That happens when our reaching out is really a reaching through the other and back to ourselves. We think we see the other, but it is only an extension of ourselves. When the other cannot meet our needs or turns out to be distinctly separate from us, the illusion is

**Sometimes
we try to secure
our own identity
by deriving it
from
someone else.**

destroyed. Psychiatrist Harry Stack Sullivan once described such efforts to support our self-esteem as ''episodes of love.''

honesty is healthy

A basic principle of mental health tells us that if we identify our own inner emotions correctly we will not be betrayed by them. The problem is that, whether we identify them or not, our emotions always affect us. Our feelings steadily influence us even if we misinterpret them, call them by wrong names, or deny them altogether. Our emotions are not a substance separate from our persons. They are not a virus that infects our personalities nor a drug to alter our outlook. They are an integral aspect of ourselves. Emotions are, as we have noted, highly informative about our identity and our meaning. When we can face them—through patient listening and watching of ourselves—we have a much clearer picture of who we are. Such self-knowledge preserves us and saves our sense of self-esteem. This is a dynamic, living understanding of ourselves that builds on our readiness to hear the truth inside us. Then we do not need protective armor when we enter into relationships with others. We only need honesty about what is taking place in our self of experience.

love to grow on

Love works when it enlarges both persons who are trying to respond to each other. Love is not really love when it drains one person completely to nourish the other. There is something badly out of line in relationships that are so distorted as to exact such a price from one partner or the other. We get into those only when we do not know ourselves and our emotions.

Real love makes room for both loved and beloved to grow. They remain separate, in possession of their own identities, mindful of their own needs, and aware of the fact that they can never merge into one consciousness. Love works precisely because people do remain separate, because their own sense of worth enables them to be distinct and to share at the same time. Lovers validate each other through the exchanges that they freely give from their own personal treasures. Maintaining their separateness, they always have something fresh to give to each other and can find something fresh in themselves. Such an exchange is the best builder of self-esteem that we know.

not facts but feelings

Lasting love has pains of its own. But they are worthwhile pains connected to genuine growth rather than the frustration involved in excessive emotional involvement. If we are in touch with the self of our own experience, we have something substantial to communicate to each other. Communication is often described as the absolute necessity for any friendship or marriage. And yet, when we inspect what people think is important to communication, we make some interesting discoveries. Some people think that if they deliver enough information about themselves to each other, that fills the bill. They tell each other where they are going, pin notes on bulletin boards, leave train and plane schedules, hotel phone numbers, and all the other necessary basic data. But that can make communication sound like covering a news story, reporting tersely to the city desk about a certain personality or event. We can do this without really revealing anything

Love
is not really love
when it drains
one person completely
to nourish
the other.

about our inner selves. We can cover the outer facts and cover up our personality at the same time. We only seem to be communicating. We are actually refraining from it without even recognizing that we are doing so.

We do not care about information nearly as much when we reveal something of our self of experience to each other. That is where we live, that is the person we really are, undisguised and unretouched. That self of experience is what is important—what we feel and care for and dream about—this is what we have to share with each other, a sense of the worth of our own experience. When we can share this, we are in communion with each other, in touch with each other's souls rather than just with each other's daily schedule.

Life can hurt us, but it does not hurt nearly so much if we have learned to listen to ourselves and to recognize how fully and richly we are trying to tell ourselves the truth. Listening to our own messages, to our own stories, reveals us as we truly are. And, in the long run, that is what we can trust and count on. The self of experience is reliable even though it is imperfect or unfinished. We can trust it and find our way into love and friendship through it. Listening to our true self is a way of really loving ourselves. And it makes it possible for others to love us as well.

CHAPTER SEVEN

Do You Still Like Me?

A lover's question, if there ever was one. We cannot survive very long unless we hear someone say "I love you." Crazy notions still arise periodically, of course, suggesting that we can do without affection and its regular expression. At times the notion of affection has been temporarily forced underground as in the cold dark days of Puritanism when, even in the way people dressed, the color seemed to have gone out of life.

But for ordinary people who maintain a good sense of what it means to be human— and what it requires to stay human—the words "I love you" remain as powerful as any ever spoken. Lovers ask the question "Do you still like me?" because they need to hear the answer. It is not just the sound of the words. We all need to feel the power that

We cannot survive very long unless we hear someone say, 'I love you'.

these words possess when they are spoken truthfully. That is why people who love each other never tire of telling each other of their affection. Such exchanges sum up what lives within us, defines what is most important for us, and allows us to feel much more of who we are.

"That means a lot," we say when someone tells us truthfully of his or her love for us. Indeed, these words do mean so much because they carry such a great weight of significance. There is almost no way to measure it because such words are living symbols when they faithfully reflect what is going on inside of us. They tell us about our self of experience and enable us to share the deepest and fullest part of ourselves with those around us.

When someone tells us that they love us, it is like sending us a check drawn on the bank of their own personalities. We know that the check is good and that it is in recognition not of some duty we have performed or sale we have made, but just of ourselves. Such a statement tells us that we are somebody special to sombody else; we are loved just for our sake with no ifs, ands, or buts. When someone prizes us just as we are, he or she confirms our existence and makes it possible for us to become more of ourselves. And we are then confident enough of ourselves to respond with the same generosity in loving. In fact, we almost burst with the need to speak our love out loud.

loving ourselves

The question becomes: *Can we give this message to ourselves?*

This does not mean that we should go through life reassuring ourselves the way a frightened boy whistles on a walk through a graveyard. Loving ourselves is not vaguely hoping for the best or, with an astrologer's faith, expecting that the signs will be right for good things to happen to us. Nor is it daydreaming or wishful thinking. Saying that we like ourselves is powerful when it flows from a genuine inner feeling of being at peace with our own existence. Liking ourselves out loud builds on knowing and accepting ourselves, assets and liabilities together.

Can we look closely enough at ourselves to recognize what is really there? Can we see everything clearly and call it by its right name? We can if we are open and honest enough with ourselves to avoid distorting or disguising excessively what takes place in our real experience of ourselves. We cannot call jealousy love or try to translate anger as enthusiasm. This means looking at more than what is wrong. Sometimes our biggest problem lies in acknowledging what is right about us. Can we be generous and forgiving enough of ourselves to let our own best selves emerge into the light of day?

Do you still like me? The question really becomes, can I like myself? And, can I like myself even though I am not perfect? Or even though I fall short of some ideal I have drawn up for myself? Or short of the one others may have proposed for me? We feel inner peace when we are content with what we find in our own selves and can settle for being our truthful selves. That is what other people like in us anyway.

being ourselves

What a relief it is to discover that we do not have to be anybody else but ourselves! That it is safe to stop trying to be somebody we are not. We are far more likable when we

When someone prizes us just as we are, he or she confirms our existence.

stop attempting strenuously to assume some pose we think others will find attractive.

If being ourselves is so good, why isn't it easy? A fair question that has a lot to do with the way we look at ourselves and the way we imagine we have to be in order to be liked by others.

We use defenses, for example, to impress others when we think that what we are in ourselves is not good enough. We fear that if people see us with our make-up off we are afraid they will reject us. We think that if others saw deeply into us they would only see what is wrong with us.

But they actually see much more than the imperfect about us. They see everything and so they can respond freely and richly to all that we are. Sometimes others surprise us by liking some of our imperfections. Lovers are always talking of the charm of their beloved's imperfections. They actually like crooked noses, misplaced dimples, and other such human irregularities. They do not like them because they are irregularities but because they belong to the whole person they love.

seeing the whole picture

Here is a key we need to understand why

others can see so much of us and still regard us with affection. Seeing all of us, they can see our faults in proportion. Our irregularities do not stand out alone; they are seen in relation to the rest of us. Taking the risk of making our faults visible robs them of the power they have when we gaze at them in isolation from the rest of us. This latter resembles looking at a large canvas only portions of which were painted—rolling thunderhead clouds, a stagnant pool, and some scattered dead leaves. If these were the only things on the canvas, it would be a stark and depressing sight.

Paint in the rest of the picture, however, adding the meadows, the blue sky, the crop-filled fields. The previous features are lost in the context of a beautiful late summer day. They no longer have the power to command our attention as they did when they were the only things we could see. In fact, we do not notice them as detracting from the glory of the picture at all. These imperfections—and what beautiful day is without them—no longer stand out alone. They look very different when we are able to get the whole painting in view. They seem to blend in, making the picture both more realistic and more attractive. Indeed the late summer day would ring false if these or similar features were totally absent. There is no scene we could view—not even that mirror into which the most beautiful person in the world gazes —where at least some minor flaw would not be visible. But overall beauty absorbs these imperfections, not by denying them, but by putting them in proper perspective.

We need that same perspective on ourselves. We have to stand back a little and watch the bad dissolve into the context of the good. Forgiving ourselves for having flaws, we can begin to see more of ourselves. We make room for our wholeness.

That is the view we give others when we take the risk of letting them see all of us; they see our faults in proper perspective. It is safe to let the unfinished aspects of our personality show through because we also allow what is strong and good and attractive to emerge.

giving ourselves a chance

Sometimes we behave like old-fashioned silent movie villains toward ourselves. We hold a mortgage on our personalities and constantly threaten to foreclose. We deal with ourselves conditionally, feeling that we

We fear
that if people
see us
with our makeup off
they will
reject
us.

are unworthy unless we meet certain specified demands. We are reluctant to give ourselves a chance unless we can meet the expectations that we make on our own personalities. So, like the widow imperiled by the villain, we live under constant threat. We become jealous or envious of others because their accomplishments seem to take something away from us. We fear losing what we already have.

We are safe from such threats when we use the best defense there is, no defense at all. True, people can see in, but, because we remove obstructions, we can see better too. We move closer to ourselves and live more comfortably there. We grow because we have a way of listening to what is happening within ourselves. We understand our experience and are no longer bewildered by it. We can face ourselves without short-changing our possibilities.

When we can make peace with our real selves by seeing ourselves whole, we no longer make impossible deals with ourselves. We only do that when we want to guarantee failure. We are like high jumpers setting the bar above any height we could ever clear. We get what we think we really deserve when we judge ourselves as always falling short. We may go through life feeling good because we feel bad about ourselves but, with a little realism and a little self-forgiveness, we can free ourselves from this punishing mechanism. We can commute our own sentence by getting at the whole truth about ourselves.

little things mean a lot

Self-esteem does not depend on huge successes. It arises from reasonable successes, from accomplishing what matches the truth about our own possibilities. Self-esteem follows when we give up living by the expectations of others and the far more cruel expectations we can make on ourselves. When we like ourselves more, we do not worry so much about whether other people like us or not.

That does not mean that we are always thinking about nice things to say about ourselves or what we accomplish. Rather, it means that we do not think about ourselves at all. Secure with our personalities, we do not need to keep retouching them or proving anything about them.

We possess the long obscured treasure, that true sense of ourselves that brings peace and contentment. The question of our worth does not constantly arise because we have settled it once and for all. We know we are likable and do not have to be hesitant or fearful that other people may suddenly discover that we possess faults or irregularities. We know that already. If we can live with them, we can be confident that others will be able to live with them as well.

do you still like me?

Do you still like me? It is a good question for lovers not because they are unsure about whether they are lovable but because the right answer sums up what is best about life itself. People who are at ease with themselves and who have given up their defenses are able to meet and share life gently and fully with each other. They like to tell each other that they love each other. They do not have to say it to prove anything anymore. But it says everything that there is to be said about life itself.